OVALHOUSE *rou.*

Ovalhouse and **Root Theatre** present

LAGAN

by STACEY GREGG

Lagan **was first produced at Ovalhouse
on 26 October 2011**

LAGAN

by STACEY GREGG

Cast

ANNE / FIONA	Kathy Keira Clarke
JOAN / AOIFE / TRACEY	Pauline Hutton
TAXIMAN / PHIL	Sean Rea
IAN / EMMET	Alan Turkington

Creative Team

Director	Jane Fallowfield
Designer	Cecilia Carey
Lighting Designer	Elliot Griggs
Sound Designer	Becky Smith
Movement Director	Kate Flatt
Movement Assistant	Jennifer Alice Malarkey
Stage Manager	Sarah Stott
Production Manager	Jane Arnold-Forster
Producer	Livvy Morris
Press	Nancy Poole
	nancy@nancypoolepr.com
Publicity design and cover artwork	Featuring Studio
Cover photo	John Annett

This production has been supported by

Development supported by **Watford Palace Theatre**

Special thanks to: Chris Till, Tom Jef, John Annett, Michael Atavar, Nicki Marsh, Rachel Briscoe and Rebecca Atkinson-Lord, Brigid Larmour and Stephanie Hay, Graham Whybrow, Lloyd Trott, Emma Dunton, Anneliese Davidsen, Wojtek Trzcinski, Grainne Keenan, Imogen Doel, Declan Rodgers, Barry Ward, Mike Bradwell, Tessa Walker, Roisin McBrinn, Simon Godwin

CAST

Kathy Keira Clarke – ANNE / FIONA
Theatre includes: *Faith Healer* (Bristol Old Vic); *Pentecost, Spokesong* (Lyric, Belfast/Rough Magic); *Spider and the Lily, The Recruiting Officer* (Abbey, Dublin); *Hamlet* (Abbey, Dublin/Lyric, Belfast); *Attempts on Her Life, Don Carlos* (Rough Magic); *Scenes From the Big Picture* (National Theatre); *Shining City* (Royal Court); *Medea* (Best Actress nomination and Ian Charleson Award; National Theatre/Glasgow Citizens). Television includes: *Flash Mcveigh, Chandler & Co, Eskimo Day, Take a Girl Like You, Pulling Moves, Silent Witness* (BBC); *Omagh* (Channel 4, BAFTA Best Drama); *Head Over Heals* (Carlton). Film includes: *Small Engine Repair* (dir. Niall Heery); *Solid Air* (dir. May Miles Thomas); *Last Legs* (dir. Amy Jenkins); *The Most Fertile Man in Ireland* (dir. Dudi Appleton); *Hard Nut* (Wiseguise Films); *Mad About Harry* (Scala); *Bloody Sunday* (Best Actress nomination Irish Film & TV Awards 2003; dir. Paul Greengrass). Kathy is a founder member of Marrillac Theatre Company.

Pauline Hutton – JOAN / AOIFE / TRACEY
Pauline trained at the Samuel Beckett Centre, Trinity College, Dublin. Theatre includes: *Brendan at the Chelsea, Christmas Eve Can Kill You, The Cavalcaders* (Lyric, Belfast); *Yerma* (West Yorkshire Playhouse); *Crestfall* (Theatre503); *Macbeth, The Penelopiad, Macbett* (RSC); *Family Stories, Antigone* (Project Arts, Dublin); *Drama at Inish, Heavenly Bodies, Iphigenia at Aulis, Translations, The Chirpaun, Melonfarmer, On Such As We, Give Me Your Answer Do!* (Abbey, Dublin); *Philadelphia Here I Come!* (Gaiety); *Midden, The Whisperers* (Rough Magic/Traverse, Edinburgh); *Tea Set* (Bewley's); *Zoe's Play* (Kennedy Centre, Washington/The Ark); *Romeo and Juliet* (Second Age Theatre Company); *The Lonesome West* (Druid); *Translations* (An Grianan). Film and television includes: *Five Minutes of Heaven* (Oliver Hiesbiegal); *Omagh* (Channel 4, BAFTA Best Drama); *The Closer You Get* (Donegal Films); *Mad About Mambo* (dir. John Forte); *This Is My Father* (dir. Paul Quinn); *Glenroe* (RTÉ); *Paths to Freedom* (Grand Pictures); *Day One* (Grand Pictures/RTÉ).

Sean Rea – TAXIMAN / PHIL

Sean studied acting at Rose Bruford College. Theatre includes: Gary Mitchell's *Loyal Women* (Greenwich Playhouse); *What A Knight* (Footlights Drama); *Compression* (Brockley Jack); *Sleeping Beauty* (Rainbow Theatre Company). Television includes: *Survivors* (BBC); *And Kill Them* (Coming Up/Channel 4). Film includes: *Chemical Wedding*.

Alan Turkington – IAN / EMMET

Alan trained at RADA. Theatre includes: *Hamlet* (Donmar West End/Broadway); *Touch* (Team Angelica); *Sweet Bird of Youth* (Dundee Rep); *A Cry from Heaven* (Abbey, Dublin); *Gates of Gold* (Finborough); *John Bull's Other Island* (Tricycle); *The Tempest/The Winter's Tale* (RSC); *The Santaland Diaries* (Union). Film includes: *Door Out of the Dark, Love, Pure*. Television includes: *10 Days to War, Holby City, In4*. Radio includes: *Journey from the New World, Portrait of a Year, Soul Music* (BBC Radio 4).

CREATIVE & PRODUCTION TEAM

Jane Arnold-Forster – Production Manager
Jane worked for many years as an IT project manager, before branching out into stage and production management. In 2010 she turned professional as a production manager. Since then her credits have included *Anna Karenina* (Arcola); *The Roar of the Greasepaint – the Smell of the Crowd* (Finborough); *Don Giovanni* (Soho). She has rallied a 12/50 Alvis around Northern Ireland since the early 1990s, so is especially delighted to be working on *Lagan*.

Cecilia Carey – Designer
Theatre includes: *And I And Silence* (Finborough/Clean Break); *Anemone* (Sprint Festival/Camden People's Theatre); *Puss in Boots* (Guildhall, Derby); *The Red Helicopter* (Almeida); *Scarlet's Circus* (Hampstead). Site-specific/event design: *The Great Train Dance* (Severn Valley Railway Steam Trains/Rosie Kay Dance Company – part of the Midlands' Culture Programme for London 2012); *Sugar Cave* (London Fashion Week); *Architectural Punchbowl* (33 Portland Place for Bompas & Parr); *The Lost Explorer* (Claridge's, London Fashion Week for Tim Walker); *Indiana Jones Taste-O-Rama* (Harley Gallery, Welbeck Abbey). Alongside undertaking her own commissions, Cecilia assists Es Devlin and Chloe Lamford on a broad range of projects from operas for ENO and Glyndbourne, to pop concerts for Kanye West, Take That and The Medieval Baebes.

Jane Fallowfield – Director
Directing includes: *Spacewang* by Tom Wells (Hull Truck /Miniaturists at the Arcola); *Burger Burger Death Burger* by Stacey Gregg (Miniaturists at the Arcola); *There is a Light That Never Goes Out* by Tom Wells (ATC/Soho/North Wall, Oxford). Assistant directing includes: *The Other Seder* (dir. Mark Rosenblatt, Tricycle); *The Holy Rosenbergs* (dir. Laurie Sansom, National Theatre); *Wanderlust* (dir. Simon Godwin, Royal Court); *The Empire* (dir. Mike Bradwell, Royal Court); *Dunsinane* (dir. Roxana Silbert, RSC). Jane runs Root Theatre with Livvy Morris.

Kate Flatt – Movement Director

Theatre includes: *Three Sisters*, *A Dream Play*, *Pains of Youth* (National Theatre); *'Tis Pity She's a Whore*, *Dr Faustus*, *Skellig* (Young Vic); *Hamlet* (Old Vic); *Figaro's Wedding*, *The Merchant of Venice* (STT Miryang, South Korea). Kate was in the original creative team at the RSC for *Les Misérables*. Opera includes: *Turandot*, *Peter Grimes*, *Carmelites*, *Gloriana*, *Requiem*, *The Marriage of Figaro*, *Carmen*, *Don Giovanni*. Film choreography includes: *The Avengers*, *Chaplin*. Dance theatre choreography includes: *The Dancing Room* (BBC2); *Soul Play*, *Songs from a Hotel Bedroom* and for 2012, *Ballroom of Joys and Sorrows*. In 2007 she was awarded a Rayne Choreographic Fellowship and is a Creative Associate of Watford Palace Theatre.

Stacey Gregg – Writer

Lagan is Stacey's UK debut. Her first play *Perve* opened at the Abbey Theatre, Dublin, in May 2011, and her play *The Grand Tour* received a reading as part of the Dublin Fringe. Stacey has commissions for Tinderbox, Watford Palace Theatre and NT Connections. She was one of the writers of *50 Ways To Leave Your Lover* (Bush/Latitude Festival/tour) and wrote a short play as part of Paines Plough's *Come To Where I'm From* season. Stacey is on Channel 4's Coming Up scheme this year and is currently developing a series with Great Meadows/BBC Northern Ireland. She has been on attachment at the National Theatre Studio and was writer in residence at RADA. Stacey is from Belfast.

Elliot Griggs – Lighting Designer

Elliot trained at RADA. He was awarded the Francis Reid Award 2011 for Lighting Design by the Association of Lighting Designers. Recent lighting design credits include: *Perchance to Dream*, *Portraits*, *And I And Silence*, *Northern Star* (Finborough); *One Minute*, *Nocturnal*, *dirty butterfly*, *Our Town* (RADA); *Drift*: *Photo 51* (Edinburgh Academy); *'Tis Pity She's a Whore*, *West Side Story* (Warwick Arts Centre); *Much Ado About Nothing* (Belgrade); *By the Bog of Cats* (NSDF 2010) and *Elephant's Graveyard* (NSDF 2009) for which he was awarded the ShowLight Award for Lighting Design.

Jennifer Alice Malarkey – Movement Assistant
Jennifer trained in Devised Theatre at Dartington College of Arts and gained a first-class MA in Movement Studies at Central School of Speech and Drama. She teaches and lectures at a number of universities and drama schools, and runs The Bear Project – inclusive creative movement workshops for people with physical, sensory and learning disabilities. Movement direction includes: research and development of three new works for UNTitled Theatre; *Richard III* (Love And Madness Productions); *The Ghost Train* (Lost); *Gut Girls* (Chelsea); *Miller* (Etectera); *Picnic, Gormenghast, On the Razzle, Othello, 'Tis Pity She's a Whore, Sing Yer Heart Out for the Lads, Dandy Dick, A Warwickshire Testimony* (Italia Conti). Performance includes: *Amphibians* (NT Studio/Offstage), nominated for six Off West End Awards; *Anemone* (ThisNowThis/Camden People's Theatre); *Renaissance Body Project* (RSC/Warwick University).

Livvy Morris – Producer
Livvy studied English and Drama at Royal Holloway, before completing an MA in Text and Performance Studies at RADA/King's College. Producing includes: *Up-Rooted* (staged readings season; Root Theatre/ATC); *White Riot* (The Space); *Crazy Paola* (Arcola); *One Night Stand* (staged readings at Soho/Riverside Studios). Livvy is currently a script reader for the National Theatre and script reader/associate artist at Soho Theatre. She also writes and performs as part of the musical cabaret act Bourgeois & Maurice. She runs Root Theatre with Jane Fallowfield.

Becky Smith – Sound Designer
Becky studied Drama at Exeter University. Sound designs include: *it felt empty when the heart went at first but it is alright now, A Just Act, This Wide Night, Missing Out* (Clean Break); *Cardboard Dad* (Sherman, Cardiff); *Brood* (Stratford East); *Frozen* (Fresh Glory); *The Juniper Tree, Reverence, The Ghost Sonata* (Goat and Monkey). Becky has also worked as a stage manager for companies including the Gate, Paines Plough, Polka Theatre, Oily Cart and London Bubble.

Sarah Stott – Stage Manager

Since completing an internship in 2010, Sarah continues to work with Islington Community Theatre as Trainee Stage Manager. Sarah graduated with a first-class honours degree in 2007 and has worked professionally in administration management. As stage manager, work includes: *Disco Pigs* (Young Vic); *Little Miracles* (national schools tour). As deputy stage manager, work includes: *Frank & Ferdinand* (Soho/Studios, Islington). As assistant stage manager, work includes: *SOLD* (Theatre503); *It Snows* (Pleasance). As stage crew, work includes: *The Beggar's Opera*, *Pericles* (Regent's Park Open Air).

root theatre

Root Theatre discovers and nurtures playwrights at the earliest stage of their careers.

We aim to produce the best new plays by writers that: have something to say, put their heart on the line to say it, and say it with a distinctive voice.

We are delighted to present *Lagan* as our first full production.

Root Theatre is run by Livvy Morris and Jane Fallowfield.

www.roottheatre.co.uk

OVALHOUSE

Anti-heroes and underdogs.
Stories told sideways.
The things under the bed.
Theatre for people with something to say.
New work for new audiences.

Since the 1960s, Ovalhouse has been a pioneering supporter of queer, feminist and diverse performance work. We remain committed to challenging preconceptions of what theatre is and can be.

Ovalhouse's current programme embodies our commitment to true artistic diversity, our appetite for experimentation with form and our dedication to process.

Autumn 2011 – Lady-Led

Lady-Led is an invitation to re-examine how gender functions as an element of artistic practice. Simply, it means that the lead artist on each project in the season is female – but the work is definitely not about 'women's issues'. The title Lady-Led itself implies a neatness, a conformity that the work explodes. This is a season by artists defining their own terms. It exists in dialogue with the idea of what a lady is, looks like, behaves like, makes work about. Gender is the context, the relevant constraint of the situation, the outside edges. We invite you to experience what is happening in the space between.

Lagan by Stacey Gregg | 26 Oct – 12 Nov 2011

Tomboy Blues by Mars.tarrab | 1 – 19 Nov 2011

TaniwhaThames by Stella Duffy and Shaky Isles | 15 Nov – 3 Dec 2011

Same Same by Shireen Mula | 22 November – 10 December 2011

Ovalhouse
52-54 Kennington Oval
London
SE11 5SW

Tel: 020 7582 0080
Fax: 020 7820 0990
info@ovalhouse.com
www.ovalhouse.com

Oval House Theatre

Theatre
Directors of Theatre:
**Rebecca Atkinson-Lord &
Rachel Briscoe**
Theatre Manager:
Aaron Lamont
Technical Manager:
Pablo Fernandez-Baz

Front of House
Premises Supervisor:
Tracey Brown
Box Office Coordinator:
Alex Clarke
Front of House Assistants:
**Ros Bird, Tex Vincent Bishop,
Justin Chinyere, Lorren Comert,
Amirah Garba, Soniya Kapur,
Michael Salami, Shavani Seth,
Melanie Sharpe, Bevan Vincent,
Emily Wallis**
Café Manager:
Barbara Gordon

Marketing
Head of Press and Marketing:
Debbie Vannozzi
Press & Marketing Assistant:
Amelia De-Felice

Development
Head of Development (interim):
Leah Whittingham

Artists' Advisor:
Michael Atavar

Executive
Director:
Deborah Bestwick
General Manager:
Gary Stewart

Participation
Head of Participation:
Stella Barnes
Head of Youth Arts:
Toby Clarke
Head of Inclusion:
Emily Doherty
Administrative Assistant:
Halima Chitalya
Pastoral Care and Monitoring:
Jeanie Reid

Administration
Finance Manager:
Tony Ishiekwene
Administrative Manager:
Annika Brown
Administrator:
Julia Calver

Board
Martin Humphries, Chair
Merle Campbell, Deputy Chair
Sola Afuape, Treasurer
Graham Wiffen, Company Secretary
Oladipo Agboluaje
Mike Bright
Esther Leeves
Layla McCay
John Spall

LAGAN

Stacey Gregg

Thank you family, Kenny, June and Christopher.

*Anna, for helping me start, Mandy for helping me finish,
Jane and Livvy for making it happen.*

Characters

JOAN, *sixty-two*
EMMET, *nineteen*
TAXIMAN, *thirty-eight*
TRACEY, *eight*
PHIL, *fifteen*
IAN, *twenty-four*
AOIFE, *seventeen*
ANNE, *fifty-one*
FIONA, *twenty-one*
TERRY, *forty-six, optional*

Genealogy

BOAL: *Anne, married to Brian, parents of Ian and Aoife.*
McKENNA: *Joan, widow, mother of Emmet and Ryan (missing).*
TAXIMAN: (*married to* THE WIFE), *son of Trevor (recently deceased) and Big Granny; father of Philip and Tracey.*
TERRY: *separated, father of Fiona.*

Note on Text

Could be performed with a smaller ensemble playing multiple parts.

Stage directions are for guidance.

At first, the prevalent force is pushing, the characters far apart. Towards the close, pulling together.

This text went to press before the end of rehearsals and so may differ slightly from the play as performed.

I. Reveille – the morning bugle call

JOAN, *warm, unassuming, in a groove worn deep into the ground by years of pacing. She walks, anonymous, carrying a shopping bag, the length and breadth of Belfast.*

JOAN   owp – (*Catching sight of something.*) awk there's a magpie – (*Sing-song.*) Two children one child – (*Stops abruptly.*) Owp…

Did I leave that friggin door unlocked – ?

She nips back the way she came, melting away…

Wind, noise…

The sea…

IAN *tests his sea legs. He is particular, youthfully hubristic. Perhaps he wears a pretentious hat.*

He has a notebook in his pocket, which he plucks out and scribbles in, intermittently.

IAN   (*Loud against the noise.*) sea behind, lean against peeling iron, salt and rust, – deck lunges, knees absorb, spray sticky on my cheek.

Someone lights a smoke. (*Miffed.*) There's only two decks, and this is not the designated smokers' area, actually.

(*Posturing, a bit grand.*) Never waste the crossing faffing round arcades or queuing for Fanta. Always spend it up here, *mysterious*, – the roar of the engine and the horizon, the upturned bowl of sky, – (*Spotting something.*) seabird! Undulating M, soaring, clockless, – (*Looking down.*) imagine the eye of a kraken, staring back up through the ocean swell…

Pulls out his notebook. Scribbles.

'Undulating M.' That's a keeper.

Wee woman staggers out, grips the rail with two white paws, squints out her crow's feet, rainmac flappin.

(*Gravelly, thick.*) 'Here love, wud ya pull that there hood up for us there.'

Sounds like a man in drag. (*Smiles, indulgent.*) 'Pull,' to rhyme with the 'hull' of a ship. Pluck her hood over her stringy head.

Dublin appears, black against low cloud, ghostly. My hands, brown against the hard white light – mad she'll think me for not just flying back to Belfast from London. God knows what's up. I'll take my time sure. Sure I've long passed caring for the relentless advice. Mother's cryptic summons, pfft – she's not the boss of me, takin my time so I am, happy to take the Holyhead ferry to Dublin, the two-hour train / north.

A well-to-do woman, ANNE, *fusses at a jewellery box. The type of woman who wears a signature brooch.*

ANNE   Balmoral, highlight of every year, marks the opening of the season for the band. Hot teas and pleasantries pass back and forth in town. Aoife was sayin –

She stops herself, fusses at something.

She changes gear, snapping brightly back, addresses herself in the mirror.

If the weather was to be fine she'd hoke out the beige flats, a steal from Clarks. Cream earrings to match. What a *coup* finding those. Fab. Oh she hoped the weather would hold up and they won't be shoved into the marquee, or worse, the church hall, the miserable church hall, dour and dark wood and folding chairs and Kit Kat wrappers screwed up behind electric heaters.

She is making a phone call on her mobile.

IAN No reception out here, brills, no one can get me.
     Should be reception-free retreats. (*Impressed with
     himself.*) Should patent that.

     Skanger swaggers out. Drops a carton at his arse.
     People actually behave like that. Maybe I've been
     away too long.

     Tannoy – 'Foot passengers to assemble and car
     passengers return to their vehicles please.' Young
     mum and her three beautiful English kids in front –

     (*Boy, husky.*) I want his hair. Mum, can I have
     Jamie's hair?

     Mum ruffles both boys' hair, setting off shoutin and
     shovin. The sister touches her own hair.

     (*Sister.*) My hair's nice, – whispery, to no one.

     Wonder how my sister is. Wee Aoife. Seventeen
     now? Mad. Haven't been home enough. Haven't
     been back best part of a year. Before that, nearly a
     year again. Too often if you ask me. I'm over it.
     Home…

     Crew prop open one door and we bottleneck,
     obedient, till some Irish voice mutters 'somethin
     somethin the other bloody door.' Spill onto the
     walkway, catch the Dart to Connelly Station.

ANNE We can endure a shower, we've played through
      worse! Sure we once started *The Plantagenets* in a
      light drizzle and didn't stop till the last minim rang
      out through a tropical storm. Very Protestant.
      People stay longer when it's outside. Something
      about being in the church hall makes people on
      edge, but when we play outside there's fresh air and
      everyone feels they're here by choice and not to be
      trapped in a corner with the pastor's wife. There are
      truisms in life:

      If you want it to be fine, it'll team (Murphy's Law)

If it doesn't rain it pours

Bad things happen in threes.

These are *certainties*. Yet she could not find the
perversity to *hope* for rain, so it would then be fine.
Besides, she isn't going to beg. Isn't going to be
held hostage by the weather, or by God. Not a bit.
Whatever happens, the band are well-rehearsed this
year, it'll be a strong start to the season. Herself,
Anne Boal, conductor, must be seen to enjoy the
day whatever the obstacles – pat round the pewter
box for the earring –

To contain her excitement, give it order, she makes
another list:

Polish horn

Buy new brooch

Call Terry to see if he needs lift to engagement.

(*Charmed.*) Sometimes Terry refers to band
engagements as 'gigs'. Like we're young things,
rock stars, like it was when we were courting and
carefree, like Yanks on TV. Ah –

She finds the cream earring –

How vulgar, – 'gig' –

– and closes the lid on it.

Terry has a streak in him. But you forgive it, for the
sake of our pattern, our lives entwined through the
lean Belfast years, for how when we look at each
other you don't see careworn adults. Babyface
Terry. You don't see the age of ones you've known
since kids. Mutual knowledge keeps youth bolted
up. It's dangerous. You begin to lean on it.

ANNE *rubs the earring, irritated.*

Tt. Film of residue grown round / the edge of the
earring…

IAN   On the train to Belfast there's a wee woman keeps
             trying to trick me into conversation, but I'm not
             havin it. Some old-boys' club banterin the girl
             serving tea. Woman opposite rolls her eyes. Ironic:
             find her just as irritating.

             (*Tea girl, broad.*) Sorry sir you really can't touch
             the tea trolley I'm sorry you really can't –

             tea girl's all dark eye make-up, fringe flat over the
             eyes, very grungy. Probably dabbles in self-harm.
             She shrugs – 'whatever'. Seen it all before this one.
             I like her.

             Yer woman opposite's asleep thank God, head lolls
             to one side, jaw juts, Darth Vader, hands primly on
             her magazine, wee prayer for Kim Kardashian.
             Cross the border. I know cos my mobile buzzes
             with the change in network. Farmland and scrag
             smudge by in silent hurry. Love this journey. Weird.
             Something about zooming through the barren,
             littered land. I've travelled a fair bit, actually, and
             the natural Ireland is divorced, irrevocably divorced
             from the urban. The natural Ireland is – answers
             something no other landscape can replace. Can't
             explain it. Maybe – maybe it is just recognition of
             the landscape of memory, childhood. Or maybe it's
             something more primitive, in the blood and bone of
             me…

             'Irrevocably divorced.' That's good.

             He scribbles it down.

             *When he looks up, he is less enamoured with the
             view. Braces himself.*

             Reel of Friesians gives way to higgledy-piggledy
             estates, corrugated iron, sporadic graffiti.
             'Sporadic.' How they always described Trouble on
             the news. 'Sporadic' – (*Rueful.*) love a good
             euphemism. Tatty flags – diagonal rain.

(TAXIMAN Taxi! Taxi! Taxi?)

IAN   Shake a leg. Train squeals into Maysfield by the
        Lagan. Take a breath. Fold my crisp packet into a
        triangle and pile the empty milk cartons / in my cup.

        IAN *disembarks and hails the taxi.*

        *The world populates, sounds of the city, urban,
        church bells, traffic.*

        TAXIMAN *wears a hands-free earset, a T-shirt
        bought for him by the wife.*

TAXIMAN – pick up some posh twat can't wait to fuck him out
        on his ear, gabblin on about the ferry and how he
        should write a book, doesn't like it here et cetera,
        whoopdifuckendoo, – some of usens like it here!

        TAXIMAN *drives, on autopilot.*

IAN   wee Aoife was always nuts, conducting music from
        the radio, takin the piss out of Mum – we never
        were allowed TV at dinner – and her baton was a
        fork and at the crescendo the fork goes flying out
        her hand, splattin on the wall – / Jesus, the mother's
        face out the steamy kitchen, hands in a tea towel,
        and us two, hysterical…

        TAXIMAN*'s speech rapid and energetic, seeking
        to enlist the listener.*

TAXIMAN I says to him no one sticks up for the white man.
        No one sticks up for the white workin man.
        Conversation-killer, but like, thing is if we just had
        to worry about the odd Chink runnin a takeaway
        that'd be dead-on. They work away, sure there's
        wee Yin Yan One-Eye been workin down the
        Ballyhack for DONKEY'S, brilliant craic, love Yin
        Yan, and he's only the one eye and Chinese, but
        y'know these Romanians or whatever, –
        everywhere now, you can't just point them out. You
        never used to get blacks over here, see – that's just
        how it was, never seen a black but on TV. We're

very cosmopolitan now. Not bad in ten years, from
Beirut to easyJet Top-City pick vegetarians all over
the place – vegetarian blacks. But this fucken
'Peace process' – loada tax-dodgin bastards up at
Stormont, two, three incomes and claimin expenses
for birdie baths and ponies whathaveye. We're busy
down here gettin annoyed at the immigrants and
slabberin over scraps when we should be astin
who's got it all in the first place. Young ones with
halfa brain still takin off d'England – tell ya even if
Philip did grow half a wit and get the grades can't
see who'd pay them tuition fees though I haven't
told him as much – I mean aye, I'm sorta my own
boss, bitta self-respect, I mean taxi-in isn't too bad
like if you can get the business, wouldn't knock it,
bettern a poke in the eye witha big stick, but nay
these Poles is on the construction – what's left of it
– jobs is short, halfa Belfast's at the taxi-in now to
get by. Jobs is sporadic. – It's hardly fucken Wall
Street, I'm hardly drippin in bling and ho's, not P.
Diddy, y'know, though I do like P. Diddy, liked that
one he did the cover of that Sting song, for when
they got Biggie – / (*Sings*.) 'I'll Be Missing You!'

IAN   headin to the garish new Victoria Shopping Centre,
           text Aoife: 'Outside.' She's the car in 'shoppin wiv
           Phil, smiley face' – Eugh text-speak. Taxi driver's
           off on one, chip on the / shoulder

TAXIMAN   Tt our Lizanne seein that bloke Tomasz – Thomas
           with a z thrown in, good at the karaoke, fucken
           brilliant Bon Jovi – but they shouldn't be
           overlookin benefits and settin the cap out. Not
           Poles though, they work away. I'm not into trouble,
           'cept maybe keepin m'gub shut when the Boys
           need, lobbin the odd brick. There was that one
           Chinese fella. Said he had someone slit his wife's
           neck. Found her floatin in the Lagan. Well, that was
           different – not like oul Yin Yan. *Bad* Chinese, he
           was. Sure a wee brick through his window's nothin

but civil duty. Then word goes round he's in the
fucken Triad! The Triad! There's only enough room
for so many gangsters, there are STANDARDS.
Fucken *level*, of acceptability. Slittin yer wife's
throat isn't acceptable.

TAXIMAN, *amused, glances in the rearview at*
IAN.

Yer man in the back's gone all bird-mouthed – can
tell he thinks he is somethin well see this is why I
wouldn't want our Philip goin off and pickin up all
the airs and graces – I know you can't get a job
wipin arses unless ye've a BA in Arsewipin and Soc-
i-fucken-ology but with us already in debt and him
not that switched on? (*Cracking himself up*.) He
comes home from school once with an Indian mate,
some Indian fella, and they'd been for a curry, I
laughs, ses to him, here, I ses, I ses sure yer man'll
be the expert, ses I, let him order yer dinner, he'll
know the gooduns! (*Incredulous*.) Everyone's so
politically correct boy, ya can't make a bloody
observation: there is *nathin* racist in pointin out an
Indian's gonna know what tastes good at a fucken
Indian! Ah but it's all boohoo this and that, can see
yer man in the back's pretendin to be on his phone –
Guardian-readin wee cunt. I'm not racist! Things
change. Nothin agin no one as long as they respect
the country. Bitta pride. Bitta self-respect. Sure even
Yin Yan ses he's near outta business cuzza
foreigners, he's been down there DONKEY'S he's
practically one of us and even HE ses it! And he's
CHINESE! If you were in America you'd be a good
fucken citizen but here it's all boohoohoo my fucken
feelins. But no one listens. I'm just the taximan.

IAN *pays and gets out of the taxi*.

IAN   Cheers mate.

TAXIMAN   Tight bastard.

TAXIMAN *flips through the radio channels, sings along at the top of his voice to something incongruous and upbeat, until –*

– Ah Christ I've to call in on my da. Tt. Christ… Turn for to go back over the humps and in and out the dusty friggin bluebells AYE MISSUS THAT'S RIGHT, A THREE-POINT TURN, ARE YER EYES PAINTED ON?

Right, stop at the corner for full-fat milk, he'll have tea, – never takes it when I'm not there, like, pretends he does. Sly. Imagine! Trevor sittin there nice as pie with a cuppa fucken Earl Grey, two sugars please – aye right – last time I forgot my Nokia and came back in he near shite – sittin there stuck to a quadruple Smirnoff. Sure, he can do what he likes. Can't teach an oul dog. One-a these days I'll come through that door and he'll be lyin legs in the air like a dead bird. Jees hope it isn't me has to find him. Took months to get our Jackie's dead eyes out of my fucken head. Every night I turn off the light and there they were the yellow whites of his eyes yellow from the booze, yellow skeleton hand still clamped round the fucken bottle like an anorexic Homer Simpson. Ahk, peas in a pod. It could be today y'know. I've come home to too many corpses. Not my turn daddio.

Maybe I'll just skip it, say I had to go on home to wee Tracey, she doesn't like bein left, gets a-scared, even if Granny's mindin them, – though she scares me too.

No. No no no no no no can't do that on the baldy oul cunt. No one deserves that. No one deserves that. See, when I watch what happens in those Middle East places and all, makes me fucken sick – if Ahmadinejad saw a poor wee drunk lyin he'd leave a footprint on his face, swear to God, the way they hang and brick the weemen and queers to death out

there it's fucken sick. Disgraceful. Lack of empathy.
If yer queer or whatever do what ya friggin want I
say: up the arse? No problem. Weemin in the army?
(Not sure, they're very emotional.) Girls wearin the
trousers, playin the golf? Why nat. Gaddafi?
Mugabe? Should be locked up. If we went to war
with the bastards I'd support it. You have to have
democracy. Standards of DECENCY. Human rights.
Ahmadinejad is not a decent man.

Whadda ya do if ya see a space man?... Park in it
man! HAH – one of Tracey's. (*Proud.*) Serious
joker for an eight-year-old. Brilliant. – See if this
was a democracy we'd've lined up every last
FUCKHEAD who drives an SUV and shot them –
off-road m'ballix – one wee bullet, DONE: parkin
spaces for everyone! Children safe. Vote for me!
Too liberal for me own good, so I am.

Right, here we go, milk, an egg, a wee chocolate
egg, take his mind off the booze for five minutes, –
grab one for the wee one, for Traceface, Philip's
alright he'll've helped himself to a Pot Noodle.
God look at the cut of it, since when did they start
employin Lady fucken Gaga to work in the Spar?
Our Philip's eyes'd be hangin out on stalks so they
would. Can she count? Soc-i-fucken-ology

– Oh shit, give me a wee smile so she did.

Awk. Nice one.

Give her a 'thanks sweetheart,' sure she's only
young. Bitta humanity.

Right, might as well dander down it's no distance.

Gettin dark. Weird bein on this street. Why the
hell'd he move back to the very street we started
in? Ates the hole o'me – Move away thirty-odd
years and this is where he ends up? Depressin.
Fucken gypsies don't even clip the hedges.

Shit. He's not brought in the post. Must be well away. Rightly already, necksprings broke. Eejit, probably passed out, like he used to when he'd come in at the scrake reekin and have us kids up and 'get that into ye, that'll warm yer uxters!' (*Laughs*.) What'd he say if he knew I don't touch the stuff? The wife likes a drink but we both know I'm a bad bastard with a drop in me, coupla shandies does me aye, no need to let on, just houl the same tin and no one'll ask, fizzy water with a lime just looks like yer on G and T's. It's like that here, no one asts but everyone'll know, good like that. Not like that cocky friggin English bloke our Lizanne brought to that party friggin astin questions like the peelers I near knocked him a new cakehole –

Up the stairs fe-fi-fo-fum this is where we used to run, oul woodchip dirty from the wee hands, fi-fi-fo-fum he'd say after you on the stairs with the lash on him and the tinkle of the buckle the clunk of a shoe and us all in the one bed.

Fuck.

(*Hushed*.) Sprawled – like he's on the

                              beach.

Da.   DA.

    cold

arm
housecoat open
wee

penis
Wee body.
Fallen   Giant. What do you do with…?
Call a… not a doctor –
Knew it'd be me. Christ why could it not be one of the others…

ENSEMBLE *breathe, relax. Quieter now. Released.*

Slippers, side by side.
Maroon. Footless.   Useless.

     Pink. White. Peach. Grey. White.

Bald skull. Liver spot. Daaaaaaaadddd – y.
Dh. Dh. Dh.
Awk
Awk
Ak

A blast of emo music.
AOIFE *turns it down. She wears skater gutties. Wrist accessories. Boysy cool.*

Night. IAN *and* AOIFE *in the car. Their patter has the quick pace of siblings.* IAN *leans over and hugs her. She is stiff as a board, though smiling to see him.*

IAN   Lights reflect bright off the wet road. Smells of roasters

             (*To* AOIFE.) Roasters for dinner?

AOIFE   (*Sniffs herself.*) Smell them, Columbo?

IAN   Glances in the rearview, headlamps slide a rectangle across her eyes

             (*To her.*) So how is everything?

AOIFE   Same old

IAN   Same old same old

AOIFE   Aye.

IAN   Don't believe her

             (*To her.*) I don't believe ya.

             She glances away.

AOIFE   (*Mocking.*) Oh I've brought shame on the family!

IAN   Thump, down like a stack of papers, read all about it.

               OTHERS *are interested.*

               Can't see much under the seatbelt.

AOIFE   it's only a few weeks. You wouldn't know to look.

IAN   oops!

AOIFE   oops is right.

IAN   Is this why I've been summoned back?

AOIFE   Probably. The cavalry.

IAN   …so

AOIFE   'so' what am I gonna do?

IAN   yeah.

AOIFE   Well, rules out zumba class so it does.

               Indicator tick-tocks.

IAN   Her hands smoothly operate this hulk of metal and plastic we sit in, us two, flesh and blood, breathing the breach in our shared lives, wondering what it means, how to talk to each other, in what language, can I still speak the code? First I've seen her drive. Notice her nails bitten. None of us were ever nail-biters – I don't know this person

AOIFE   I have to get rid of it y'know.

               A beat.

IAN   The 'It' sits between us. 'It' dangles from the rearview like a scented tree. Look ahead, not wanting her to feel scrutinised. I never – have to admit this – never properly thought about abortion, was all Freedom This and Save the That at university. But the possibility of a life, a being, a fucken soul – She reads my mind –

AOIFE   I know. I know it's –. I know it's – / it's y'know…

IAN   bites her lower lip, the way she did if we'd been
           sent upstairs and the parents were havin a barney,
           voices burring up into our mattress suckin sleep
           away and Aoife bolt upright, lip-chewing at the
           foot of my bed.

           'Wee Aoife' up the duff! What do I say? Say it's
           okay? Do I believe that? She could've waited,
           Jesus, coulda waited till I'd got in the door before
           dropping that bomb, Jesus. *Inconsiderate*. The
           drama. 'Welcome home' – and there'll be the
           parents, shadows in the window jookin out the
           blinds at the sound of a car. But. But I think how
           she's had to go back to that, night after night. And
           I'm annoyed for getting annoyed. Slime of family,
           sliding back into your childish self

           (*To her.*) Is he around?

AOIFE   the da?

IAN   aye

AOIFE   No.

IAN   Whatdeya mean 'no'

AOIFE   (*Lightly.*) Haven't told him. Parents think he's out
           of the picture, had his wicked way with a wayward
           slapper

IAN   alright, God, too much information

AOIFE   Dad thought it was Philip at first, ridiculous

IAN   *Phil?* Isn't he like seven?

AOIFE   He's fifteen.

IAN   What're you doin sleepin with people anyway – you
           should be at school colourin in seeds or somethin.

           AOIFE *gives him a withering look.*

AOIFE   I'm just not interested in his input. It wasn't…
           havin a baby'd be wrong…

IAN	– maybe ya shoulda / thought of that
AOIFE	God don't lecture, not you too, don't go / givin me crap
IAN	no I didn't – . I'm just…
AOIFE	Well.
AOIFE / IAN	(*Quiet.*) I don't love him / she doesn't even love him
IAN	She's the heating on full blast, sweat. She chews a finger at a junction, riding the clutch, car swaying gently back and forth – nauseating vision of some man chewing her finger, holding her down, pullin at her, her – I, I rub my eyes. She didn't even love him
AOIFE	Don't be feelin sorry for me.
IAN	Listen to our breathing, the rhythmic wipers, the rain.
	I should write this down. Reminds me of my year in Africa / actually –
	They are suddenly pushed far apart. Time has rushed forward.
AOIFE	push a stupid fish finger round my stupid plate. Total. Pompous. Dick. Slam the door in his face, thunder up the stairs, aren't enough doors to slam – Bastard, *lecturing* about abstention in Africa, fucken *lecturing*! And is he wearin *tweed*? YOU'RE TWENTY-FOUR FOR FUCKSAKE! The Mother's face like a cat's arse, closes her eyes, Mother bloody Teresa, collects up warm cups and retires to the kitchen to make as MUCH NOISE AS POSSIBLE, Dad turns up *MasterChef*. Heart's a fist. Talk to me! Talk about it! Talk to me! / Ask me!
IAN	Aoife's eyes are grey, always remember them as more colourful, / green-y
AOIFE	Shut the fuck up Ian, shove yer notebook / up your jacksie

IAN   She wears make-up now like cool grungy girl from
           the train, they could be mates, / start a band

AOIFE   such a hypocrite, mummy's boy, if she only knew
           why you're never here any more…

           Morning.

           *They consider, calmer. Both in their own parallel
           train of thought.*

IAN   Okay.

           Truce. Morning sun slices through the blinds, warm
           stripe, through one of Mum's many dreamcatchers.

AOIFE   Tt, she'll hold up some lump of flippin TWIG on a
           string in front of ya and wait for praise –
           'Dreamcatchers' – freaky little witchy / things

IAN   burnt the toast and it hangs in the air, sweet and
           bitter. Aoife's eyes glitter. Home. But not home.
           House has that breath-holding when everyone
           should be at work. No one was ever out of work in
           this family. Can't remember last time we sat, in the
           day, in our house, just / us two.

AOIFE   Last time we sat here was when we both had the
           shits after Granny cooked us / chicken.

IAN   If I do this, I'm choosing between Aoife and
           parents.

AOIFE   Do ya want a flippin Oscar? Get over yourself. Just
           help me. It's not *Sophie's Choice*.

IAN   Mum hasn't even mentioned it. I don't even know
           what I – things shift and pop around the quiet tubes
           of the house. A baby in her

AOIFE   (*To* IAN.) I've got the money

IAN   It's not about the money.

           I try –

           (*To* AOIFE.) How's Mum?

AOIFE   Won't talk to me. Not really dealing. Still
recovering from Balmoral, eejit, she'll talk to you
but, golden boy.

ANNE   Roused herself, to call about Terry's lift. Phone's on
one of those wicker reception tables in a nest.
(*Tickled.*) It's tradition to pick Terry up, she and
Brian picked up Terry for their own wedding, as
Terry is fond of telling people.

Anne's heart fluttered and she forgot what she was
doing. Making a cake? Yes baking a cake –
(*Excited.*) everyone loves a cake, and thus a cake-
maker. Cake-baker. Everyone would marvel,
everyone would say, mmm Anne, that's a fabulous
cake, did you – ?! No. Really? *No.* TELL THE
TRUTH, awk I thought it was from Marks &
Spencer! DELICIOUS! – Yes a cake for the band!

Pigeons out the back garden, picking over crusts.
Pigeons spread disease – RAP the kitchen window.
(*Proud.*) Ian, visiting from London – where he has
a really spacious flat, – has made an Ulster fry, left
the place a bombsite. But she didn't mind, typical
boy just, he'd eaten well, just needs a wife. Just
needs to meet the right woman.

A moment. EVERYONE *fidgets, looks off.*

She's not worried about him. Has to keep an eye on
the cholesterol anyway, even if he *had* offered.

Unfurled the cloth to burnish her horn, dab dab of
Brasso polish, the pungent odour, takes her right
there, to the past, that smell, oh reminds her of the
days of big competitions, heyday of the band, Terry
in the front row and Maggie and Claude and Jimmy
all like a line of soldiers, smart and purposeful,
ready to go over the top for their country, their
district, instruments shining like suns. Spit-spot.
Loyal soldiers. For God and Ulster! Can't say that
now but awk no one was as *sensitive* then. Then

there'd be drinks. Cigarettes. *Carry on.* Not now of course. Now it's watery tea and a Penguin if you're lucky.

There's the young ones to consider in the band now, local kids farting down mouthpieces. Lord but it's unbearable. Recruited them herself. Trudged round schools and searched for what's become a rarity: talent. Commitment (gave up on Aoife long ago, the incident with the trombone and the gerbil put paid to *that* – wilful girl, why on earth would she do that?) – Were we *really* novices once ourselves, purple welt on the embouchure? – but Band was a source of pride. It was our gang, (*Temperature rising.*) and we were bl*ody good. This new blood want to be pop stars and unrealistic things with unrealistic bodies all over MyFace, FaceSpace, Spacebook – no one tells them it isn't likely. These days it's all follow your dreams and LIES. Hussies and sluts. Hussies and sluts wilful wilful.

There is one young talent, Siobhan, sullen one, used to sit next to Terry, made a fuss to move into the back row, away from Terry – (*Irritated.*) unnecessary fuss, doesn't look like she's the puff to fight her way out of a paper bag, but when she sets those lips to the flugelhorn... never heard the like. But ach, always absent from rehearsal with some sickness or other, starey thing, dark eyes boring into you, slippery. Not like her own direct offspring. Weeper too. If there is one thing Anne cannot abide it is a weeper! Makes her want to lash out. Even Aoife grew out of her whingy phase. Children are so soft these days, soft as boiled eggs, not like her own strapping Ian, all twelve stone of him, making his fry with capable, man-hands, breaking eggs and cursing, not even pausing to fish out the shell. Girls are different. Loose. Cats. Whores. The phrase 'bun in the oven' crossed her mind but she punched it out of the cake mix below la la la.

The phone rings.

AOIFE *answers.*

A voice.

AOIFE *freezes.*

The OTHERS *watch.*

Anne created the cake from muscle memory. For a second, she remembered Siobhan's mother, waving limp hands, gesticulating about some 'nut allergy' – the woman was too much, vulgar. Anne's fist hovered, crushed almonds and brazils peeping between the knuckles, and release! – showering nuts as spring rain onto a garden – Oh it would be a lovely day for the band with the sun already scratching through just beyond the kitchen window la la la!

AOIFE *slowly hands* ANNE *the phone.*

ANNE *won't make eye contact with her.*

TERRY'S VOICE	Hello?
ANNE	Of course of course! I was just about to call, you read my mind Terry.

Raspy laugh. That's just Terry. All the men smoked, it wasn't bad for you in their day, things weren't bad for you then. You got on with things. Now everyone is watching, commenting, telling you, everything's bad for you now – (*Getting angrier.*) too much cake, not enough cake, cake if you're pregnant, tea with cake, CAKE ON YOUR HEAD God knows. God knows these things were once a luxury. Too much of everything is the problem with young people.

Terry took an infection last year, time off from the band, and Anne had suggested he give it up now. Just, take it easy, wouldn't that be a grand idea? At the time, some in the band intimated maybe it was time to lay the euphonium down.

Whispers. Eyes.

AOIFE   (*Flat.*) No one said it straight out, no one looked each other in the eye, but some enquired, would Terry *really* be up to coming back to the band?

ANNE   (*An undertone of defiance.*) But he did. Bounced back, in his cream Dexter, brogues, twenty Silk Cut in the shirt pocket, hands always jingling change, fistling, fiddling. Apart from when he's playing. He's a wonderful euphonium. Takes the solo in 'Wind Beneath My Wings', and in the arrangement of *Titanic,* written especially for the band by the late Rev Walters.

Perhaps the strains of a euphonium.

Safeway supermarket.

TAXIMAN *and* ANNE *in a queue.*

FIONA, *younger, perhaps seventeen, excessive foundation, bored, works the checkout.*

(FIONA   Beep. Beep. Beep)

TAXIMAN   Years ago in the queue at Safeway, me and the wife're discussin the closure of the local sandwich shop 'BAPS' – (*Helpful.*) as in tits – turned out the owner ran a porn ring, found hundreds, *thousands* of images on his PC, *wild* images –

(ANNE   Anne eavesdropped, dimly repulsed)

TAXIMAN   so wild, people couldn't even finish the sentence, couldn't even find the words for it and if they could then they were as bad as the dirty pig! The wife never liked them fucken sandwiches, – and sure you know yer man TERRY, aye, apparently he's a dirty fouterer an' all!

A chill.

ANNE   Anne's thoughts tripped flat over the name and lay
            stock still.

            FIONA *tenses, looks away.*

            Express checkout, dragging her forward, towards
            judgement, – Anne laid out her soda, milk and
            tomatoes very, very carefully. Beep. Just *talk*, so it is

(FIONA   Beep
            Beep)

TAXIMAN   Yer woman in front takin ages – (*Recognising her.*)
            Boal, aye, lived down our street when I was wee,
            her ma looked after my granny when she was
            ailin…

(FIONA   Beep)

ANNE   Beep. Receipt. The couple behind distracted,
            unpacking the trolley. Home free. Purse clip.
            Leave. Bury!

OTHERS   *The cake!*

ANNE   The oven door clanged and there was just time to
            POLISH THE HORN! Anne meticulously poked
            into every crevice, rubbed and buffed and burnished,
            – if you aren't careful, blackness will spread from
            the bits that are hard to get at. Oiled the valves,
            played a couple of trills. Let out the 'lake' they call
            it, bastardisation of 'leak' in the old Belfast lilt. Ran
            herself a bath. Washed herself down with a soft
            lemon cloth. Massaged and scrubbed. Rinsed down
            the tub, and sat back on her knees, looking in. Bath
            stared back at her, white, oddly expectant.

            Two o'clock, pull up to Terry's door with the
            clouded glass, his daughter Fiona, pretty thing if
            she'd put a smile on, wear less slap.

            FIONA *leaves, barely throwing an upward glance.*

            Perhaps AOIFE *watches.*

Two-thirty arrive to set up metal stands, stiff from the cold. It's always the good ones who turn up early and give a hand, – the young ones tend to get dropped off late by parents who don't even stay for the performance. Girls are the worst.

Somewhere, AOIFE *soundlessly mouths 'Mum. Mum. Mum?'*

Unheard, she retreats.

Behind my ears starts to ache from the smiling, beige flats and cream earrings, – why not reveal the cake now? Someone passes comment on my brooch. Lovely brooch Anne. Awk thank you, just sitting around so it was. Worried my cake will only get lost, when it could be appreciated now, a celebration, – isn't done to eat before playing, but then, I won't have any myself, and it wouldn't be that they *have* to, it's more the gesture. Produce the Tupperware, peel off the lid, position it…

(*To the gathered, casual.*) Oh just a wee cake there. Just had it lying about the kitchen, so I did.

And they gather round, murmuring and crumbling, sugar fingers complimenting, loaves and fishes loaves and fishes – No no, I wouldn't even take a cup of tea: I'm fed by the watching of everyone else mill about full and happy. I am on cloud nine.

Church bunting twitches. Anne leans over to pick up a stray clothes peg, useful for pinning music, – breeze kicks up her jacket, circles her neck, snatches a napkin through the air, landing twisted in the damp grass.

EVERYONE *shivers.*

Something is wrong. But something is wrong now.

Why are people moving quickly?

A stand knocked over, clattering on concrete,

sprawling across the semicircle. Anne's reflex is to fix it, fix it upright, – but what is happening? Feet rushing across gravel, swarming to the flugel section, someone on the ground, Siobhan, convulsing, someone raising their voice for an ambulance. Everything is wrong. Anne pushes into a voice demanding,

(*Shrill.*) What's in the cake?

Were there NUTS IN THAT CAKE?...

IT WAS HER OWN FAULT THE SILLY BITCH!

An intake of breath. AOIFE *looks up sharply, disappointment across her face.*

ANNE, *breathless.*

It's out of her before she knows it.

Somewhere, AOIFE *turns her back on her mother.*

A hail of nuts.

Anne, dead in her tracks.

Anne, lists obliterated.

Anne, frozen. Anne, guilty as charged. And just at the corner, a figure, smoking by the church...

OTHERS   Terry, smoking.

ANNE, *finally letting it in.*

ANNE   (*Private, upset.*) silly bitch.

JOAN, *that wee woman with the sensible coat and shopping bags, in her groove worn deep, looks up. Pauses, clears her throat.*

She addresses us directly: JOAN *is between worlds. She is full, matter-of-fact, robust.*

II. Narked

JOAN   ah there's more between Heaven and Earth, y'see,
            they're always there, perched on our very chests.
            Do we listen?

OTHERS   (*Sing*.) 'One finger one thumb keep moving,
            One finger one thumb keep moving,
            / One finger one thumb keep moving,
            (*Quiet, suspended, melting away*.) We'll all be
            merry and bright'

JOAN   – aye, we talk of the future, the rise and fall of
            house prices, (Owp look a wee starling) but
            between the blink and the breath they're gabblin.
            Everywhere has ghosts, but we've them comin out
            our friggin ears, – in rows along the worktop,
            leakin out the washin machine, crushed in the
            laundry basket, spoonin in the cutlery drawer

            JOAN *walks in her groove.*

            (*Sing-song, with each footfall*.) Two children, one
            child – a tick, makes me walk like I'm walkin the
            tightrope, one after the other two children one child
            – the length and breadth of Belfast.

            JOAN *boards a bus, back in her own world.*

            Bus windows dark with an ad on the outside of a
            smiley shoppy woman.

OTHERS   She looks out through the laminated woman's
            forehead, a third eye, as they cross Queen's Bridge.

JOAN   people SHOCKED about the weather, and sure last
            year the sun was *splittin* the very trees. Used to coo
            to Ryan in his buggy, bright eyes closin and openin
            up at me. Losin shoes, pullin toes (*Sing-song,
            amused*.)
            The wind blew
            And the snatters flew
            And my wee dawg was cut in two!

OTHERS   Fat clouds trail over a spire, spillin sun down the
           Black Hill wet glass and steel, / blindin.

JOAN   The changeability's shackin, ya can't / keep up!

OTHERS   Nigerian bus driver pulls down his sunnies, hoots at
           a Micra, wee tot in the back seat flicks two fingers.

JOAN   Most weemin look the same, practical coats and
           short hair.

OTHERS   Corner of Joan's crucifix catches the glare and
           reflects like a lighthouse from her chest, and she
           watches the outline of her own face staring back.

JOAN   Bus noses into Laganside, one of the oul rattly buses,
           brown and hard inside, not the flash new ones that
           hiss and drop for disableds. Come for to have a keek
           round the new Victoria shoppin complex off Anne
           Street, though I don't need for anythin.

           Weave past the Albert Clock, prostitute on the
           corner, legs eleven, – cut through the arcade at
           Mountpottinger – oul posters with Closing Down is
           all's left. Shoe-Rack Everything Must Go. Things
           change, I know, them Shoe-Rack shoes were hot
           off the back of a lorry, cracker – ah but these days
           we're discouragin the Boys from all that carry-on.
           Reignin in what over the troubled years was
           normal. Wouldn'ta bat an eye once, like when
           Emmet wanted a camera, or an ounce, it was only a
           matter of askin the Boys to sort ye, week later
           someone calls and ya fix a price over a cuppatea.
           Things shift faster than you can fix them. I'm a
           mammy, I should know. Set a toddler down one day
           and it'll ask you to pick up Rizlas the next, set the
           skitter down one day and he'll fall in with the
           wrong crowd, get himself…

           JOAN's voice echoes, her steps echo.

           It's only the *rate* of change… Apartments springin
           up along the Lagan, owned by wee Jimmy from

The Corrs, well they bring in money, there's worse
than wee Jimmy from The Corrs – (*Thoughtful.*)
though he's away in the head, ses 9/11 was aliens…
pass a preacher in Cornmarket…

Strains of a brass band. JOAN *shivers.*

thought I heard a brass band.

Everything stops abruptly. A face.

(*Chilled.*) A face – pale orb watchin me through a
window – shakin its head – big ears, big jaw. My
reflection over his: both faces mine

OTHERS   Tears her eyes away. Blinks hard like a cartoon.

Turns back to a blank window. Empty shop.

Disappointment is it? Which is better: he be still
there, staring like that, or that it's a nothing, a
nothing at all.

Her eyes flicker over the crowd, gauging the mood,
steadying the heart, pushing it down. A ginger in a
Celtic top sneezes. Plastic bag tumbles away.

JOAN   Waves of hope, hurt, can happen any time: the
hairdressers', mass, waiting at traffic lights – the
middle of a bloody zebra crossing near Pizza Hut,
they thought I was a boogaloo. Kids have no
patience. Scunnered. Not their fault, it's outside
their understandin. What it is to have borne a life.
Young uns'll never have patience with the old, till
they themselves grow old

two children one child…

She looks up sharply.

God have mercy!

SHAPS!

Tiny men buff glass risin out a pretend street and
up, up, – queues travel up and look from the

observatory over Belfast, past Samson and Goliath
the two yella shipyard cranes holdin up the sky, and
on to where the green hills lie belly up. Sway on
my Hush Puppies. WOW! They built a whole
friggin street! And I'm gawkin like a simp!

JOAN *holds court.*

*Low-level shopping-centre pop muzak creeps into
the air.*

ANNE *and* IAN, *having tea in a café.* IAN *in a
cardigan.*

ANNE   Looking awful Londony. Wish he'd cut his hair.
            Stir my tea.

IAN   Try to talk. About Aoife. Everything. She's off about
            some twat's hair off a TV show. Glossing over.

ANNE   My boy. Son. – Not here. Can't be / makin a scene

IAN   Suddenly see it.

            Fear. Me, doing exactly the same.

            Aoife was always more like Dad.

            Stir my tea ask me I mean, I've got a man bag. /
            Just ask.

ANNE   What'll people think? Of Anne? – (*Gasp.*) there
            goes Joan McKenna used to clean Mum's nursing
            home, looked straight at me, probably thinking
            'he's awful long hair!' – I did my best! Shove my
            white-chocolate raspberry muffin in my mouth, /
            Eat, Stir, Deflect, Push on!

JOAN   Shoppers drift above, delirious. Prayers have been
            answered. Husbands tugged by wives with fierce
            to-do lists give in to posters of men in cardigans,
            dangerous and fresh from London, where all the
            men wear cardigans

            – feel like I've had a go on that there wacky baccy
            Emmet's always smokin. Only ever tried it the

once, sure all the boys do a bit of it, just felt giggly
and polished off a bag-a-Jaffa Cakes.

Glide up the escalator and watch a wee niknak strut
by the illuminated fountain, throwin shapes like
he's a TV under each arm. Security point up where
only kid's balloons hung, now, rows of CCTV,
watchin, watchin. The lad returns from whence he
came. His sort's to be relocated. (*Compassionate.*)
Poor lads, what'll they do now?

A New Belfast, aye.

A kinda emptiness hangs but, shiftin round corners.
Sure everythin's designed spartan now. Redistribute
my bags. Lookin up is like flyin.

Looking up, her smile freezes over.

GLASS! – SKY SHATTERIN!

JOAN *shrieks and covers her eyes, bags spilling,
coins tinkling off the balcony.*

TAXIMAN *silently annunciates something in her
face, a reassuring hand on her back.*

JOAN *opens her eyes…*

…man with his wife, astin me somethin. No glass.
Nothin. (*Embarrassed.*) Pretend to look for
somethin.

A memory is all it was. A ghost: see, years ago at
Castle Court, just down the road, the loudest bang
you ever heard. Loud as a cannon. Storm of glass.
There'd been a bomb warnin from the IRA. Just the
loudest, the *loudest bang*. These things take root,
live on in your darkest mind, your night-time mind.
There's no use tryin to discipline ghosts. That's all
it was sure. My eyes're just tired with the lookin.

JOAN *heads for a café.*

A tea'll fix it. A tea'll settle me. It's good to have a
goal.

Sounds distort, amplify. JOAN *catching her breath.*

Only now my skin. Like someone's turned the sun off – the ring of cutlery, thump of bodies, eyes – a baby cry pangs with more than hunger.

Go away down a deserted bit to catch myself on. Shops still under wraps, scaffoldin, bend to set down the bags that've got heavy.

An unearthly shriek. The OTHERS *look up, horrified, screaming.*

Somethin yanks my eyes up – a blur –

(*Calm.*) The face was Ryan.

The face in the shop.

Never found his body, never knew what happened. Had he survived? Lived in secret? Why hadn't he contacted me? Why –

(*Understanding.*) He's dead. And he's here. To warn me…

OTHERS   (*Flat.*) CCTV captured the accident. The woman wandered into a cordoned-off area, became pinned by falling scaffolding.

(Joan McKenna, sixty-two, beloved mother of… one? Two?)

No point showing the footage to the surviving son, Emmet McKenna, escorted to the morgue, tea and half-eaten Rocky Robin discarded on the kitchen bench. No one to tell him she died with a smile.

The song, 'two children one child', somewhere. JOAN, *elated, floating higher and higher.*

JOAN   Ryan, buried deep in the foundations, warnin me off, or beckonin? That ditty I sing, two children one child keep movin, did it call out to him? I'm high in the dome. I'm the view, terraced houses, the apartments, murky Lagan and Cave Hill, timeless, witness.

The rest of you will get by.

Quiet. Long quiet.

JOAN *in her coffin.* EMMET*, back to us, silent.*

JOAN *whispers with a masculine energy, feverish, ventriloquising* EMMET *and his energy. It doesn't matter if we can't quite hear her.*

Knuckles resting on the corner, overpowering lilies.

No more. Emmet wrestles with it.

The hands would be bound together by the rosary, hadn't looked that far. Strange, the shite y'look at on the internet. Maybe she's hoverin above right now, somethin outta *Ghostbusters*.

EMMET *glances up.* JOAN *watches her son, peacefully. Clock ticks.*

Silence. Dog barks.

Upstairs someone flushes / the toilet.

EMMET   haven't shat all day.

JOAN   his aunt in the shadows – sedated – admires how gentle the big lad is, and thoughts swim away.

           A man's quick sob, deep in his chest somewhere not felt since a wee boy, and only when alone in his room. It's the sight of his aunt's loss bunched round her puffy nose that pierces the scary numbness, more than the dead. The dead's dead. They're okay,

JOAN /   they're dead.
EMMET

JOAN   Here, by the sunken lips that wouldn't say 'son', he feels sorry as he ever has for anything.

           He usually has an excuse.

           This is the first absolute Emmet has encountered.

Is he one of these there psychos doesn't feel things? That's what they'd called him at school. School was kill or be killed. Emmet done both. The old howl fills him, but scampers away and swallows itself.

Wakes should be livelier, someone should've cracked open the flippin Guinness! Relatives ferry in and out with condolence faces, Clinton Cards, remember a black-eyed schoolboy causing his mammy headaches – (*Disapproving*.) 'You'll go like your brother.'

Buries his body like a bone in a corner.

EMMET   At least she's happy nay, with Ryan.

JOAN   I am, son, but frigsake I miss *you* nay.

EMMET *turns at a noise.*

TAXIMAN *respectfully drops off* FIONA *and* TERRY, *a word for* FIONA, *a hushed hand on her arm, himself grieving for his own loss.*

TAXIMAN   Dust in the wind, love. Dust in the wind.

FIONA   (*Brisk*.) Terry McWilliams fancies himself a man of business, though everyone and their dog knows he's a euphonium-playing wanker. Wrapped in his Dexter, proud silver hair, comb in his pocket, hands-free phone, like some kind of city banker, – all it does is confirm

TAXIMAN   he is a first-class wanker. No one knows what he does, and he's told everyone somethin different. In that way he's clever, gift of the gab, spoofer. Bitta this bit of that. Type of cunt who records quiz shows so he can play them back when people drop by, let on he knows all the answers.

FIONA *appears, steely, striking, impenetrable.*

FIONA /   Eyes.
EMMET

OTHERS *sit up.*

FIONA   (*Rapid.*) Eyes bright: freckles, lips – one of those
          piercings in the inner ear, make-up – jinglin coins,
          fairy bells. From under his hair he wonders how a
          wanker like Terry could've produced a girl like
          this. Terry?

OTHERS   Jesus

FIONA   she was probably a bitch but. Her nose probably
          stuck up, and the jinglin? Tt. Fixin her make-up,
          waltzing in here, *jinglin*

          EMMET *shifts, drawing the girl's attention. She
          smiles.*

          blood pumpin round his...

          EMMET, *covers his crotch.*

EMMET   peripheries.

          The wanker bletherin in the kitchen, huggin
          m'aunt, – I'm awake, poppin like a lemonade
          poured. She's in profile. (*Whisper.*) She's lookin –

FIONA   (*To* EMMET.) Sorry.

          EMMET *struggles to remember how to speak.*

EMMET   For what?

FIONA   For your mam.

          He half-shrugs, gives up on the shrug, gives up
          gesturing altogether.

          Sweeps the floor with his eyes, shoring up.

          (*To* EMMET.) Y'lookin after your auntie?

EMMET   Think I'm a baby? Belly's at a rave. Maybe this is
          grief? She turns toward the casket, more lovely
          neck! Hands meet on her lap, somethin written in
          blue Biro on the back.

          (*Full voice, soft.*) Want to see her?

FIONA   I – . Yeah. She always asked after Mum. I work
          down the road in the chemist, she'd come in,
          y'know…

          Pad over to the body. Emmet spying.

          Elsewhere, a TV murmurs horror films.

          TRACEY, *playing behind a couch. Some moments
          of play. She is sparky, cheeky, precocious. She gives
          herself to us fully, usually speaking a hundred miles
          an hour.*

TRACEY   Musty in here but (ohmyGod if you sneeze and
          don't close your eyes your eyeballs pop out like an
          egg from a chickenarse) I LOVE behind the couch!
          CONGRATULATIONS. YOU SURVIVED THIS
          TIME! Monster outside growls – DON'T LET
          THEM EVEN KNOW YOU ARE HERE OR WE
          ARE FINISHED, DEAD, MINCEMEAT, FISH
          FOOD! I love chocolate eggs so I do, push 'em
          away and pretend you don't want it, then you'll get
          one, – like grown-ups, just pretend you don't want
          them then they give you a hug – I love hugs so I do
          I GOT IT ALL WORKED OUT!

          Shushes herself.

          Listens, to see if anyone has heard.

          No one can hear over the film anyway. Granda
          Trevor and Granny's *separated*. He's just dead but
          anyway, away to Heaven, donno if he'd want to be
          there but, Mum says there's no vodka there. Big
          Granny doesn't have eyes in the kitchen, her
          glasses are blank under the bulb BANGS the door
          to the yard where monsters are and a murderer will
          be CUT TO SHREDS if he even *tried* to get in –
          flopped over the wall like a dead doll guts dribblin
          – don't go down there Tracey, Granny ses – she's
          fulla – (*Whispers, giggly.*) shit but, I sneaky up
          there and dance hee hee. Granny ses I've the touch
          of the devil so I do!

EMMET   At least when there's a corpse involved no one's in
            a rush.

            She looks straight into me.

FIONA   You okay?

EMMET   Question into the bottom of a hole, shield my eyes
            – Terry spills into the room. She touches my arm –
            does a wanker sign towards her dad's back, fucken
            snort so loud m'aunt scuttles out the kitchen.

            The chemist's. Beep. Beep.

            Fiona.
            Her name is. And turns out Fiona does work at the
            chemist. Fiona, it says on her badge. FIONA blue
            embossed on white acetate.

FIONA   Turns out Emmet's run out of toothpaste.
            Beep.

EMMET   Coincidence.

FIONA   Drops it on the counter, nonchalant. What? Rounds
            his lips to whistle, thinks better of it. Can't fix his
            face back. Pretends he always does this. Just a
            quirky thing he does, right? What?

EMMET   Hi.

FIONA   Hi. (beep)

            one forty-nine.

EMMET   Wha?

FIONA   That's one forty-nine.

EMMET   One forty-nine?

FIONA   Yeah

EMMET   drop a fiver.

FIONA   Scrutinise receipt

            (*To him.*) Bag?

EMMET   Wha?

FIONA   Bag?

EMMET   (*Garbling*.)
             Shake head, no,
             pocket   FIONA   Look how his
             toothpaste. Wait   eyes burn, the
             for somethin,   swagger. He's
             anythin. Give her   *shy*. Is that CK
             all the time in the   One? Bit
             world. Say   nineties. The
             somethin. Why   boss, Sandeep,
             doesn't she say   leans on the
             somethin? Is she   counter. At the
             a fucken idiot?   scent of a flirt the
             But her hair's so   mouth'll be
             clean, silver   flappin. Want to
             necklace across   know how the
             her throat. But   funeral went, if
             she's up herself.   he's okay, do
             So far up herself.   people usually go
             To come here, to   shopping for a
             be treated as a   single toothpaste?
             customer. We've   Say somethin, say
             a *corpse* in   somethin! He
             common.   doesn't even
             Doesn't that   notice me. Beep.
             mean something?   Beep

FIONA   If it hadn't been an automatic door I'd've slammed
             it.

                                  *

             EMMET's *prayer:* OTHERS *hum, religiously.*

EMMET   (*Liturgical*.) Oh God please please oh please your
             beauty on me Fi-oh-naah better than the comput-
             aah!

             From devotion to restlessness.

Day looks different through my big new heart eyes
bang bang bang, don't think of porn, no way, too
pure, fuck World of Warcraft!

Back at work since the funeral, up at half-six,
usually be asleep. Why can't I sleep? Some big
private house in Ballyclare, landscapin with Kieran
– *Oh lovely lovely Fee-oh-naaah* stoned at work,
spin out, hummin The Ronettes – hard-house remix
YES – smilin like a fucken gluebag – toothpaste!
Can't shake this radiatin from my chest, shovellin
dark earth, scrapin stones, edgin turf. Kieran's
lookin at me funny.

(*Kieran.*) What's wrong with ya?

nothin.

(*Kieran.*) Me hole, you've just worked three hours
straight without a tea break or even a whinge!

I MUST'VE BEEN DEAD BEFORE!

*

EMMET *and* FIONA, *in bed, together.*

FIONA /	She's an animal to him.
EMMET	He revulses. Slag.

She's an animal to him.
He revulses. Slag.
His hands stop. Curl into themselves.
Worse, he turns from her.
He turns bodily away.
She's blasted by this, his back. Shorn stump.
She holds him though.
She holds him with her.
And it's okay for you? her eyes ask.
His jaw pops.
He is reconstructing his god, cracked in pieces all
round the bed. Picks up a fragment: this is where
he thought he might even be her first.
In the chill of after, he's disappearing, brutal.
But she holds him here, firmly. She picks up a bit
and slots it together. See?

She'd let him find his own way. He was controlling
and gentle. Then she'd met him, guided him. In the
moment, all he'd wanted was to reach together,
and she was there too, they were reaching and it
was like nothing he'd ever felt.
But now her concentration bothers him. The rising
up together bloomed, passed, and now drains as
the cool air cools their bodies. She was powerful.
He's annoyed. He was not her first, clearly, far
from it.
She's reading his face intently.

FIONA   *Fine, be like the others. But I think you're different.*

FIONA /   She's still holding him. Her biggest fear is him
EMMET   rolling away, now. Now of all moments, the most
               vulnerable.
               Look at me

                    Look at me

               She traces his eyebrow, his cheek.

FIONA   *Grow up Casanova.*

FIONA /   He's reordering. Replaying. It's all so new.
EMMET   Her heart skips a beat, she drops away from him,
               pulling in, protecting herself. He feels her gone,
               panics, looks up.
               Wait, his face says, *I'm getting there*.
               She's pulled the corner of the sheet over herself.
               He looks into her face, an abyss of shocking
               closeness, and moves beyond shame. Beyond his
               self. He's beside her again. They breathe together
               again. The room becomes warm. Possibility in the
               gap between their noses. In the inch, the birth of
               love.

                              *

               JOAN *averts her gaze, considerately.*

JOAN   Earth – Emmet blows on the mud dark half-moons
               of his finger ends, and claps. Reverberates flat

across the Ballyclare garden. Cold work. Fresh.
Sweat patches from his pits. Life before Fiona. No.
It had never existed. He didn't exist before this.
Thank you.
Thank you
thank you
thank you

*

TRACEY   Creak goes couch and – (*Exaggerated laugh.*) HAR
HAR HAR! scarin me where I wee from, I'm the
only girl in this damn family, this *damn* family *I'm
the only doll*, *shucks* only one has to sit down on
the stupid toilet. It's too loud the laughin, like a
Lambeg. Not normal laughin like when someone
falls over or puts ice cream up their bum ha ha ha.
If Philip laughs more I'll have to wee but I can't
but cos the fever-dogs'll get me, Morlocks, Daddy
callsem, – love my dad, he lets me sip his tea from
a china cup. Daddy talks Chinese with Yin Yan
'Suplise Tlacey!' Told me he brung the cup from
China himself with two beautiful whores. Daddy's
out in the taxi makin a crust, Mum works nights
and we be good for Granny.

TAXIMAN   (*To himself.*) No time for grievin, gotta earn the
crusts, the bling an' bitches.

TRACEY   Wish he'd come home, bring me a chocolate egg.
And kung po noodles. Terry give me a quid for
noodles when I was with Mum in the club. Terry is
SO STUPID, a quid's not enough for kung po
noodles. CAST AWAY! AHR AHR ALL HANDS
ON DECK! THARS A STORM A-BREWIN!
Secret stowaway – if I get caught we'll be scalped,
fed to dolphins! Trapped under the couch, crushed
to death by Philip's gigantic MASSIVE ARSE
OhmyGOD it's too late – *Killed in action!*

TRACEY *executes frantic, ostentatious hand
signals.*

And some more.

STAY BACK! WAIT FOR THE SIGNAL! THIS
BITCH IS GOIN DOWN!

FIONA *and* EMMET, *spooned.*

FIONA   Hold you, in your *Transformers* duvet.

EMMET   Her grip's cool.

FIONA   (*Steely, curious.*) Sense the shudderin damp.

EMMET *hides his tears.*

(EMMET   Mam)

FIONA   Didn't realise you're cryin, thought you were with
me, y'know? Keep you inside, stroking your back,
your arse. Breathe you in.
Jack and Rose.
Baby and Patrick Swayze.
Shrek and Princess Fiona.
Emmet and Fiona, y'know?

Stories. Escape. The 'Troubles' – myths and
legends as real as Finn MacCool, the tooth fairy.
I've been searchin. You wanted found. You've
fucked, whatever, but never like this, y'know?
Okay I've had a fair few, but my heart's never been
in it either, it meant nothing. Fuck all. I was *lookin.*

EMMET   Honesty, she's just being honest. I'm a stranger to
honesty.

FIONA   You look so funny in the buff.

EMMET   Fuck you so do you, look like a Moomin.

FIONA   (*A smile.*) Come with me.

Your eyes search, *why do you like me?*

Cold, I get called. But you see past it. You're warm
– (*Wonder.*) makes me warm. He notices, now the
make-up's off. It's hardly vanity. It's camouflage.

Something in me knows you'll turn away one day, maybe. But now's not the time, y'know?

Thoughts judder on your hip bone... black-and-white image: skinny white bodies, hairless, like aliens, emaciated, piled like twigs. Dachau. Can I understand this much? No.

All this talk about there being a *way* people behave, nature or whatever, people hurt and covet and desire, learn to suppress. At the bottom of everything is cruelty, y'know? I'm not a pessimist, but there aren't any reassuring rules.

She turns away.

Being Terry's daughter taught me this. Can't hate Terry totally, fucker that he's been, cos I am him, in different skin. It's in me. Once you've drawn your own blood you can live with this:

EMMET *brushes her scars, scores along her arm, hidden. She recoils.*

she looked into a Gorgon face
and hasn't turned to stone.
One punch made me distant.
Two punches made me invisible.
Three punches make me invincible.

Everything is still.

EMMET *coaxes her back to him.*

(EMMET   Come back.)

FIONA   (*Thawing.*) but there's now. There's you. There's the wink in a taxi driver's eye, and kids who know and fear nothing, and the softness of the woman's voice asking if you want a wee bag with that

TAXIMAN   (*Gentle, matter-of-fact.*) dust in the wind love. Dust in the wind. Make the most of it babe. *Carpe diem* like.

FIONA   I deserve you, put up with Terry and didn't kill
          anyone, didn't rip off his head and feed it to
          birds... don't know why, but I trust you... words,
          words, crap. Orange night rolls into dawn, waste
          our lives wishin to be someone or somewhere else
          and then spend the rest of our life wishin we were
          back there again. Eejits. Dirty big fry sizzlin out the
          back of the launderette, bass from a passing car,
          millions of possibilities and, here.

          The sound of joy. Pigeons, The Ronettes.

          This town's pock-marked with stale fairytales. But
          there's dying all over. What do you do with it? Sink
          or swim?

EMMET   We're swimmin away on an IKEA bed. To The
          Ronettes hard-house remix.

FIONA   Huckleberry and Tom on a raft and the bells chime
          across the city for joy.

EMMET   Up up dive the cherry blossoms and everything
          steely glitters like a sea.

III. Ambush

TRACEY *mimes sexing.*

TRACEY   I seen *The Candyman*, *Scream*, *Terminator*,
           Predator, *Silence of the Lambs*, *American Werewolf
           in London*, *Shutter Island*, *Kill Bill*, *The Ring*,
           Psycho but ohmyGod I HATE the sexing.

           TRACEY *mimes sexing again, with gusto.*

           That's what happens in films. Even if it starts good,
           it always ends up being about SEXING. If there's a
           film right and there's a boy there'll be a girl and if
           there is it'll totally end doing sexing even if the
           world is about to blow up. And the Boys're just so
           lying if they say they like it cos ohmyflippinGOD
           it's just so BORING. Don't understand why they
           ruin everything with it – Philip is such a bumhead,
           he wants to do the sex on Aoife he says he asked
           Santa for a bazooka and reckons he's gonna get it,
           he got a grenade last year, savin it for when Dad
           really annoys him, hide it in his Coco Pops.

           The movie kicks off. TRACEY *shrinks.*

           COUCH HITS AN ICEBERG – IT'S SINKING
           WITH ALL WHO SAIL ON HER. Film's screamy,
           door BANGS: that GAY smellbert bumhead dog is
           bouncin off it
           Bang.
           Bang.
           Bang.
           Bang.
           Bang. Pause. (PAWS! Ahhaaaah!) – that dog is
           such a bumhead! Sulkin cos Big Granny beat him
           with the brush Granny was a milly in the
           ropeworks. She made ropes. Granda was a docker.
           (*Making it up.*) He uhhh made ducks.

           (*Huffy.*) Granny-hands make me wear clothes I
           DON'T like, pointy shoes I DON'T like and hair

done wrong in frizzy plaits I DON'T like –
(*Wistful.*) wish wish the hands would reach for me,
turn out the light put soup on a tray don't splash,
want them hands to see me. Pay attention, look for
me. Find me! I'm not comin out okay!

The TV gets screamier.

Everyone hides from it.

TRACEY *gets more nervous.*

Just wait a few years and I'll be the *X Factor*. I'll
be so important and everyone'll listen. Everyone'll
notice when I'm lost. When I could be dead, identi-
fible only by teeth. Identi-fible only by a ribcage.
Right now I could be, like – anythin – murdered,
crushed under this EFFING couch, last will and
testicle – I've been here FOR EVER and i could be
DEAD.

Try it out, death.

Mimes being a corpse.

Some moments.

It's okay.

Suddenly TRACEY *laughs her head off, hardly
able to tell us why.*

Philip farted!

– HARHAR laugh again. What's so FUNNY –

Look at the TV:

She watches the TV, mouth agog.

this man has something in his mouth. Coconut is it?

Ball?

Why's it in his – ?

An explosion on the TV.

TRACEY *gapes*.

Grenade! In his mouth
exploded him
to PIZZA
!
Hands lift me please please please yuck sweaty
dark stingy nasty BOKE – I've completely DIED
here and no one will save me! PUKE – hide like
the dog I've died here like the man in the mountain
Daddy?
Daddy?
Da?
D?
Oh
Ohmmmm mnnnnnnnn mmmmmmhHHH
DADDY!

TAXIMAN *comes home and scoops* TRACEY *up in his arms. She clings tightly to him.*

He kisses her, murmuring, reassuring, and switches off the TV.

He shouts at PHIL, *clips him across the back of the head.*

PHIL *storms out.*

TAXIMAN, *cools, repentant.*

IV. Ur text: growing up

AOIFE *and* PHIL *kicking about, if at all, in circles.*

PHIL *frenetically checks his mobile phone, force of habit. They constantly exchange phones, on which videos play.* PHIL, *fidgety, trying to be well hard and cool. Maybe wears his hood up.*

AOIFE	Milky sky sags against the / hospital
PHIL	Tt faint siren / woooOOOOo-oop
AOIFE	Tt. Why do we hang out here Phil?
PHIL	The craic? An' your mum has the car. Lucky Strike. Crouch, suck a fag.

PHIL *really milks the cigarette smoking.*

Check out that one Aoife – 'ten balls in one face.'

Hands AOIFE *a video to watch.*

Cows hang over Hawthorne, slurry, hospital parkin, dual carriageway fadin out of town past lone McDonald's. Glad to get outta the flippin house, tt can't do anythin right at the minute, don't know what's up with Dad like!

(*Feverish.*) Was inspired to take up smokin, actual smokin is like whatever – gross – but I *look*. Like. AWESOME. Bettern a haircut. Smoker's cough is mega sexy. Purchased m'first twenty, big man. Excited.

The ritual of the fag:

Flick the pack on the bottom, eject fag from top, tap it on the box. Tap tappity tap. Magic. Tap tap tap. Light… Drag. Magic tap tap. Saw Splicey do it after school. Amazin. (*Inspired.*) So much I'm gonna do. This is just the start!

AOIFE *laughs as the clip ends.* PHIL *loads another video.*

Puff and practise, flick my hair. Flick, pat. Flick
pat. Flick pat. Abracadabra. Puttin everythin into it,
Aoife, will ya notice me here for fucksake.

She spits chewing gum, expertly caught with
Reebok, sails into some oul biddy's hair.
(*Admiring*.) Class. Better 'n GCSE revision, which
sucks massive dicks. Who gives a flyin fuck about
photosynthesis? Just electrons and some shit.

PHIL *dumps his revision textbook in a bin or shrub
or whatever.*

AOIFE   So gay.

PHIL   (*Hurt*.) wha?

AOIFE   You. Chain-smokin.

PHIL   Homophobe. You're gay, ya slabber.

Gob – another new habit. She thinks I'm well cool,
I can tell.

AOIFE   (*Critical*.) Hasn't the hang of the gobbin yet. Spot
brews on the bridge of his nose. Hectic. Why's he
acting like a weirdo? Supposed to be my best mate,
BFFs. Want to talk, like we used to. Head's
spinnin –

PHIL   Sunday
Sunday
Fucken. Boring. As. FUCK.

AOIFE *dismisses the latest video and hands* PHIL
back his phone.

AOIFE   That one's not funny.

PHIL   What's worse than a maggot in your apple? Gang
rape.

They both suppress a snicker.

Church bell somewhere. Mime drummin.

He air-drums, with commitment.

Pretty good like. Could probably do it professional.

AOIFE   (*Hesitant.*) I've to go to London next week. With Ian. To do somethin scary –

PHIL   – Cool – I want to go to Vancouver so I do – Canada's coolern America – pop the butt through the air – into scrub – *Psst*: awesome.

AOIFE*'s hand strays to her stomach.*

AOIFE   Phil?

PHIL   (*Hopeful.*) Wha?

AOIFE   Nothin.

She tries to speak again, but nothing comes out.

PHIL   Been standing here twenty fucken minutes of my life. Love me love me love Aoife – fuckit – lay a decision, hit the footpath –

(AOIFE   We goin?)

PHIL   – she follows skip hop. Tries to keep up. I'm on a roll –

(AOIFE   Milkshake is it?)

PHIL   (*To* AOIFE.) I wish – flick my hair. Pat

AOIFE   What?

PHIL   – wish somethin, y'know, would just like, happen, to me.

AOIFE   What like –

PHIL   – bein raped, or somethin. I just wish like –

AOIFE   Someone would rape you?

PHIL   Shrug, small words flutter.

(*To* AOIFE, *styling it out.*) Yeah whatever. D'y'know like? Mental.

AOIFE   I'd rather have a milkshake, like.

            AOIFE *backs away hand on stomach, a gulf opens*
            between them.

            She waves goodbye, goodbye.

            Tannoy. Seagulls.

            AOIFE *and* IAN *on a ferry.*

            They're playful, messing around.

IAN   the air rings with the laugh of my sister, pissing
            round the arcades, staggering as the ferry heaves.
            Every time Aoife goes to put a coin in, I nick it out
            of her hand

            (*To* AOIFE.) givus it

AOIFE   No way!

IAN   Givus the money if you've enough to be throwin
            away!

AOIFE   Get yer own

IAN   I'm minted

AOIFE   Cos ya travel Tightarse Ferries, steada flyin like a
            sane person

IAN   Low carbon footprint –

AOIFE   Low carbon knob. No one to spend it on?

IAN   just number one.

AOIFE   Know what you need?

IAN   wha?

AOIFE   a baby.

IAN   Sick!

AOIFE   You laughed I saw ya

IAN   did not

AOIFE   did too

IAN   C'mon if I win a million I'll give ya a tenner.

I leave her, queuing for Fanta in her big mingin green fleece, take up my post on deck, different to the person stood here a week ago.

He stares. It's incredible.

stars are insanely bright, sea blacker than tar. No one else up here: bitterly bitterly cold *Mir ist kalt. Du bist so dumm.* Thinking in Stefan's voice, he'll be waiting up for us getting in. Left on an argument. Said I hide behind words. (*Defensive.*) I said he was projecting, actually, I don't hide. (*Deflating.*) He said, why do you avoid going home.

(*Mortified.*) Am I a cliché? Think I need to get through to Mum.

School exchange with Stefan, only my German tutor then, stood, maybe this very deck, side by side with him, imagined my illustrious escape on the horizon. Funny to be here now. Me and Aoife.

AOIFE *appears behind, unnoticed.* IAN *gazing up.*

Lose myself, mind unravels in sudden collocation with other times I sky-gazed – feel all these selves at once, the particular bursts, dormant muscle, a fist releasing, palm upwards in the present

(AOIFE   some night, there's the Plough)

IAN   shoot into galaxies, luminous shreds hurrying across eternity

The OTHERS *follow his gaze.*

seas move and crash and slide, and I'm catapulted into the impossible *here* and *now* and the heart beats out, a whisper –

OTHERS   Come:

          The sound of joy.

IAN   'Life. Live' fills my ears – and at the same time
          death, non-being –

(AOIFE   mad, isn't it, the sky)

IAN   the glimpse into the sublime when all the shit's
          quiet and everything's nothin, – but already it's
          sliding, retreating, strapped down by words, my
          mind ordering.

AOIFE   Probably composin a fucken sonnet or something,
          get offside before he tries it out on me.

          AOIFE *wanders back in.*

IAN   It's gone. Sudden as it filled me, leaves a residue in
          my gut as hot as booze, sharp as the frozen rail.
          Inside, a stir, lust for love and what? Kids? More.
          Something. Wish Aoife was out here. Should check
          on her.

          And I've lost it, the mind goes skipping to
          mundane things, and there's no use chasing.

          Spot Aoife, leaning by a window, condensation
          dribbles by her head, little legs. She's watching a
          woman talk to a wee boy, making him laugh –
          Mum takes a sip of Guinness and lets the head
          collect on her lip, looks at him innocently. He loves
          this game. Probably the funniest thing he's ever
          seen. Aoife laughs when the boy laughs. She
          looks… beautiful.

          AOIFE *looks beautiful. Does she wipe away a
          tear…*

          Weird. Since I got home I see a woman, not my
          stupid wee sister with the sausage baton. She's torn
          her cup into shreds. I do that.

          (*To* AOIFE.) Alright?

AOIFE	brilliant.
IAN	Slurp. Burn tongue, bastard. (*To* AOIFE.) beautiful up on deck
AOIFE	Freeze the tits off a china doll.
IAN	I was just, y'know, thinkin.
AOIFE	Wow, – need a lay-down?
IAN	Just like… are you sure –
AOIFE	Not now. Please. Just not now.
IAN	but
AOIFE	please please please let me just get through today okay? You can't just decide to talk about it like that. I wanted to talk about it earlier and you didn't. This isn't actually about you.
IAN	Sip my coffee for something to do, but my tongue's killin me. Look around and wonder do they know it's an abortion boat. She draws a cock in the condensation. Can't she take anything seriously?
	AOIFE *painstakingly draws a cock.*
AOIFE	(*Suddenly.*) 'member the arguin when you came back from college?
IAN	Aye.
AOIFE	There was me, fourteen on a search for God, like ya do, and you come fannyin back denouncin organised religion all over the place.
IAN	didn't think she'd taken any of it in, didn't think she read a newspaper / let alone –
AOIFE	You swan home lecturin. Do you still believe all that? Or not believe. I mean. Like. Where do you 'stand with God'?
IAN	Fuck. Tread careful. (*To* AOIFE.) I wouldn't say I'm an atheist.

AOIFE   Agnostic like?

IAN   If you're putting labels on things

AOIFE   Just answer for once, Ian. I'm a pantheist I reckon.

IAN   (wha?)

AOIFE   Like, believing in the world, nature and like –
(*Searching*.) stuff. I mean…

IAN   and I listen. I actually really listen.

AOIFE   If you were to give me some good stuff about souls
I couldn't really handle it, I really couldn't,
specially from you who put the doubt in my head in
the first place. Cos when you boil it down, that's
what separates them who'd call me a like,
murderer, from like, practical.

IAN   (Burn tongue again)

AOIFE   So I need to know. (*Holding it together*.) I'm shittin
myself here. I need to know which one you think I
am. I have to know it's my right, even if you're not
allowed at home. But that's cos of the Church and I
don't – it wouldn't be kind to have it. I really want
kids, but not yet. I want to actually love them and
give them a proper home. You worked in
Mozambique, – so many poor things, dyin…

IAN   Set down the coffee. Don't think I can hug her.

    (*To her.*) How could you stay here?

AOIFE   (*Beside herself.*) How could you leave?

    He takes it in.

IAN   – but – I – I don't know Aoife.

AOIFE   Well think. What do ya think I've been doin?
There's pills off the internet or there's payin out a
grand and doin it this way. Think this is easy? Have
you any idea what people are like about this?

IAN   I – I just think if you'd been forced, or there was
             something wrong with it we'd be in different
             territory but – ahm...

AOIFE   Do you think I'm a murderer?

             A beat.

IAN   She's gone. Pushing past people in the gangway,
             away from me. I did that. Made that girl cry. Cos
             I'm too stupid to say the right thing.

             Somewhere, AOIFE *passes* TERRY*, catches her
             breath, recoils.*

             A breath.

AOIFE   You left, apologisin. Had a shower. Liked not bein
             a virgin.

             S'alright. Bit lonely. Bit euphoric.

             Had a baby in me but. Not so great.

             They stare at one another.
             TERRY *stares at her, conflicted.*
             AOIFE*, unsure of herself, but fronting it.*

             My decision. Always my decision. Don't flatter
             yourself, Terry.

             A breath.
             AOIFE *sweeps away.*

             A park. Birds.
             EMMET *and* FIONA *pass, hand in hand.*
             TRACEY *shows off cartwheels.*
             TAXIMAN *reads a tabloid.*

             AOIFE *on a bench.*

ANNE   Air still and rich with falling leaves.

AOIFE   On a wooden bench along the Lagan towpath.

TAXIMAN   Tracey's the pockets filled with twigs already. She's
             a wild passion for collecting fucken twigs so she
             does.

AOIFE   It's quiet, early, joggers o'clock.

Won't tell Mum about Terry. It'd tip her over, go
bananas so she would…

She composes herself, waving.

Spot Ian. Sun halos his hair, dog lead dangles, poor
fella, will he ever just come out, even Dad says it,
so nineties, doesn't he watch *Hollyoaks*? And he's
the cheek to worry about me? Now bestiality, that'd
be controversial, give the curtain-twitchers
somethin decent to jizz over. At least he's happy
over there, with Stefan ze German.

He points to Percy squatting behind grass.

TRACEY   OHMYGOD CUTE DOG!

IAN *flops down beside* AOIFE *in the sun.*

AOIFE   See Mum and Dad?

IAN   Aye.

AOIFE   They okay?

IAN   Yeah. Getting there. Mum gave me a pair-a gloves
for ya, case you were cold. Said she'll be up in a
bit, they're just behind me.

AOIFE   Gloves?

She takes them, surprised. Checks them out. Smiles.

When you goin back to London?

IAN   Not for a while…

AOIFE   Cool. (*The dog.*) Takin the dog for a run?

IAN   Yep. PERCY! C'mon you –
See ya later.
Good luck.

ANNE *approaches, uncertain. She's been
collecting twigs.*

ANNE   She's sitting in the sun.
            Sit next to her. Terrified. (*A trace of her old tone,*
            but without the edge.) Where she got the
            willfulness from I do not know…

            Eventually my eyes close, head tilted back, face a
            cup taking in the heat.

            Blink in and out of nothing, blissful as a sunning cat.

            AOIFE *turns and realises* ANNE *is there, eyes*
            closed. She puts on her gloves.

            Above Stranmillis the sky's azure, cloudless. Only
            sound's birds in the dry leaves and my breathing.

            AOIFE *eyes the twigs in* ANNE*'s hands.*

AOIFE   Dreamcatcher?

            ANNE *discards the twigs, letting them drop to the*
            ground between them. A smile.

ANNE   Awk, I'm not very good at them.

AOIFE   I like them.

            AOIFE *bends, picks up the twig, holds it. She leans*
            back again, eyes closing.

            Makes ya dizzy

ANNE   The sun?

AOIFE   (*A bit overwhelmed.*) Yeah, all the stuff.

ANNE   I'm nodding like a nodding dog. Nod nod nod in
            the sun. Which is funny, because she can't even see
            me, her eyes are closed too.

            AOIFE *breathes.*

            ANNE *breathes.*

            Someone hums JOAN*'s song.*

            And out of frame, TERRY.

            The End.

A Nick Hern Book

Lagan first published in Great Britain in 2011 as a paperback original by
Nick Hern Books Limited, 14 Larden Road, London W3 7ST,
in association with Ovalhouse, London

Lagan copyright © 2011 Stacey Gregg

Stacey Gregg has asserted her moral right to be identified as the author
of this work

Cover image: John Annett/Featuring Studio
Cover design: Ned Hoste, 2H

Typeset by Nick Hern Books, London
Printed in Great Britain by Mimeo Ltd, Huntingdon, Cambridgeshire
PE29 6XX

A CIP catalogue record for this book is available from the British Library

ISBN 978 1 84842 231 5